Identifying, avoiding and conqu
challenges in Six Simple Steps

MONEY MYTHS

AND

MONEY MISTAKES

…as seen on *Moneywise* with Kelvin Boston PBS Series (2006)

Take control of your personal finances by changing your mindset and learn to organize for success!

www.moneymythsandmoneymistakes.com

PIRAAS® LLC Publishing
PO BOX 3093
ALEXANDRIA, VA

For more information address PIRAAS®,PO Box 3093, Alexandria, VA 22302

Book Design by Dennis T. Comer and friends

Library of Congress Cataloging Number: 2005904814

Comer, Dennis T.
Money Myths and Money Mistakes/ Dennis T. Comer

1. Personal Finance 2. Self Help 3. Nonfiction

ISBN 978-0-9767408-0-3 (e-vers)
ISBN 978-0-9767408-1-0 (spiral)
ISBN 978-0-9767408-2-7 (perfect)

DEDICATION

This book is dedicated to the people who have had the most impact and influence on my life.

With deep gratitude and love this book is dedicated to my family, immediate and extended, for being strong, independent and true to their own dreams. Most of us have managed to guide our life in a manner that works without reliance or burden on the other family members. However, it's always those few family members who can't get their money right that inspire me to write this book. I personally want to thank everyone, who did or did not "handle their own business" for their inspiration.

...and to my other family, those who are called to the profession of arms....HOOAH!!!

Dennis Comer

CONTENTS

PREFACE

I have been working on this book for a couple years with the intention of providing personal finance insight for soldiers. I never mentioned my endeavor to my family. When I thought I had enough text to show the makings of a book, I decided to call my mother and ask her if she would review what I wrote. "You're writing what" she asked? I told her I was writing a personal finance book. She immediately went on to point out how ironic that idea was considering I had immediate family members who had filed for bankruptcy not once but twice! That led me to consider the fact that although military life has a unique set of financial considerations, it seems the general public could also use a helping hand in the financial literacy arena . I decided to broaden my focus and develop a book that will benefit everyone.

One of the greatest things that happened to me in my military career was being assigned to the northern Virginia and national capitol region. Not for the sake of my military career, but it was there that I was exposed to the roles and functions of non-profit organizations and the great works they do with little to no funding. It was during my assignments in that region, that I became exposed to and involved with organizations that worked for the greater good of the community. It is for the people, who struggle despite insurmountable challenges to do all they can to provide a better way of life for themselves and their families that I write this book.

INTRODUCTION

Have you ever:

1. Wondered how you got into your current financial situation.
2. Wondered what you would do if you had a few extra dollars.
3. Wondered how some people never seem to have any money problems. (not wealthy folk...people you know)
4. Wondered what you should be doing with your money.

It is common knowledge that the most important things in life are not taught in any school or classroom. Things like: How to be a good parent or boyfriend, How to love someone unconditionally, How to manage money effectively. For these, some of life's more important topics, you are basically left on your own. My question to you is: How do most people learn these things? Before answering, let's think about this for a second, where did you learn your money skills? The answer is...people usually learn by emulating what they see or hear and then attempt to process the information in a way meaningful to them. Well, when it comes to your current money skills, it is probably those early influences you are emulating, which may be contributing to your current money problems. Early experiences with money, good or bad tend to have a very lasting effect. If those experiences are negative you will have financial difficulty until you realize there may be a problem and then commit to doing something about it.

It is time to look at some of the more common myths, notions, and sayings about money and determine what is really going on! Believe it or not, most of us are victims trapped by our own thoughts. Reading this book and following along with the worksheets will help you to break free. You will escape those past mental demons which have been preventing you from accomplishing what we all truly want - financial freedom!

In this book you will be exposed to the many possibilities that can lead to financial organization and ultimately financial freedom. Stay alert because if you blink you might just miss out on how to overcome myths, notions, and sayings we all hear and/or use concerning money. After reading only the first chapter, your OUTLOOK about money will go from negative to positive instantly! We will examine how different notions may subconsciously influence you. Consequently, you will develop a method to use these myths, notions, and sayings to be on a fast track to financial freedom.

Now, let's get started

First, to complete the Worksheets provided you'll need:
Pencils
Erasers
Notebook/Folder
Calculator

Optional but **highly** recommended:
Computer
Financial software

I know this is only the introduction but this is serious business. This is **your** business! The above list of materials is no joke. Please go get them right now. You will begin using them in the next chapter.

At the end of the book are blank examples of all of the worksheets. I suggest copying the worksheets and using a folder to keep track of all your materials for future reference!

CHAPTER 1 – MONEY MYTHS...

So what is money? What is it about this thing we call money that is making people so crazy? How do you learn how to control and manage this thing called money? I believe how we deal with money stems from how we think about it and the value we place upon it. What I hope to accomplish is to alter you mindset about money. To do this I would like to introduce you to a couple of friends who will help us out --- Joe Knucklehead and Susie Smart. Joe and Susie are going to show you how they think about money and how it is affecting their lives. Now close your eyes and take a deep breath.

So what is money? Simply put, money is nothing but a tool, not unlike any tool you would use to fix your car, build a house or plant a garden. I would like you to think of money as if it were a hammer. Let's examine the hammer for a minute. What do you use a hammer for? You use a hammer to build things. You use a hammer to drive nails to fasten things together. That hammer has a specific purpose and when used properly it can help build very strong foundations. Can you use a shovel to drive nails? Yes you can, maybe, but it would not be the best way to build something. It will probably take more time to accomplish the same thing you could by just using the proper tool -- the hammer! Money, too, is a tool. You use money to build things. Money has a specific purpose. There is a proper and an improper way to use money. Can you use other things to accomplish the same purpose as money? Yes, maybe, but you can accomplish so much more if you learn how to use your tool - money better. The more skilled you become with your hammer the better the things you will be able to build. Have you ever seen the work of a master carpenter? Just think of the things you can build and accomplish in your life if you become skilled at using money. Let's see how Joe and Susie use money as a tool in the following scenario.

> Joe and Susie have just been hired at company ABC. It is their first jobs. Joe and Susie both take the bus to work. Because they rely on public transportation, they can not work over time (no bus service at night). Both Joe and Susie decide to buy a car so they can make extra money by working over time.

How are Joe and Susie using money as a tool? Both have decided to use money (from their wages) to purchase a car. By doing so, they can both take advantage of working overtime thus making additional money. So both Joe and Susie are using money as a tool to purchase a vehicle.

The next concept I think is important about money is *how* it is used as a tool. Long, long ago before there was money, people needed a way to get the things they needed. People needed a place to live, they needed food and they needed clothing. So how did people get things? They traded or exchanged for them. A fisherman could trade his fish for other foods, clothes or maybe shelter. People would trade goods (things they owned or had) and/or services (things they could do). The common name for trading goods or services is bartering. In most countries today people still barter over the costs of goods and services. Haven't you seen in the movies where a person is in the town marketplace haggling over the price of some trinket with the merchant? That still goes on today, although it is not as greatly practiced in the United States.

Money was established as a common "tool" everyone could use to exchange for the goods and services they want. The money could be in the form of gold, diamonds, coins or paper, but it is usually in a form that everyone recognizes and accepts. How would you feel if you had a t.v. to sell and someone offered to pay for it in chickens? How many chickens is your t.v. worth? Would you even accept a payment in chickens? Could you in turn go buy the things you wanted with chickens? Of course not. That is the role of money! Now, a person can sell their chickens at the market and receive some money. They can then use their money to buy your t.v. What would you rather have their money or their chickens? The purpose of money is to provide a common method to exchange good and services. It is this money that you can use to acquire the goods and services you need to best suit your life goals. Remember, the better you learn how to use your tool - the proper way - the easier it will be to accomplish what you wish with that tool.

My Grammy used to say...

Below is a list of common money myths, notions, and sayings. Some of them you will be familiar with, others will be new to you (fig 1.1).

Worksheet 1 - Sayings

#	SAYING	+	-
1	A bird in the hand is worth two in the bush		
2	Money makes the world go 'round		
3	A fool and his money are soon parted		
4	Money is the root of all evil		
5	It's only money		
6	Money doesn't grow on trees		
7	Money doesn't bring happiness…		
8	Money can't buy love		
9	Money talks and BS walks		
10	Don't put all of your eggs in one basket		
11	Show me the money		
12	The buck stops here		
13	Don't throw a good quarter after a bad nickel		
14	A bad penny always returns		
15	Money burns a hole in your pocket		
16	Put your money where your mouth is		
17	Knowledge is power but money pays the bills		
18	Don't be penny wise and pound foolish		
19	Don't nickel and dime me		
20	Cash is king		
21	Another day, another dollar		
22	Money follows money		
23	Neither a lender nor a borrower be		
24	I got my mind on my money and my money on my mind		
25	Watch the pennies and the dollars will take care of themselves		

Fig. 1.1

Are we victims of our own thoughts?

Time to grab your pencil and go through the list. As you read each saying I want you to place a checkmark:

In the "+" column if you believe the saying is a POSITIVE OUTLOOK to have towards money or
in the "–" column if you believe the saying represents a NEGATIVE OUTLOOK towards money.

Do you know of a money saying that wasn't listed? Add it to the bottom of the list and place a checkmark in the column you feel best represents your OUTLOOK of the saying.

Now that you have decided whether each saying was either a positive "+" or negative "-", I would like you to TOTAL the number in each column, write it at the bottom and keep those numbers handy.

POSITIVE "+" OUTLOOK

Those sayings that you feel are positive "+". There is no reason to address and/or change. If you believe they are positive then I bet you are using them in a positive manner as you manage your financial issues. Is the number higher than the "-" negative, if Yes, you are on your way to financial freedom, if No; we've got some work to do.

NEGATIVE "-"OUTLOOK

Next, we are going to take a look at all of the sayings that you marked with a minus "-"; these are the ones you feel represent a negative OUTLOOK towards money.

Putting this into practice, for example, I feel that the saying:

'***Money burning a hole in my pocket***' is negative "-".

Why do I feel that I have money burning a hole in my pocket? Is the money itself actually burning a hole in my pocket? Perhaps it is the notion in my head that I just have to spend any money that I have not allocated to something else. The fact that I have any money in my pocket should be a good thing!

Wait! Before we go on, I want you to think about this for a minute. "Money burning a hole in my pocket." Do you ever get that feeling? If you are like me, you only get that feeling when you "fall" into some extra money. You know, like during tax season when you get a bigger refund check than you expected, win money in the lottery or when a repair costs less than you thought but you already scrimped and saved the money to cover the expense. How about when you get your apartment rental deposit money back - all of it!

Whenever you are surprised by having extra money, are you suddenly eager to spend it? Why? Is it because you believe:

1) You are not entitled to have it in the first place or
2) Lucky to have it and so you must get rid of it as quickly as possible.

Let us examine Joe Knucklehead and Susie Smart and their money

1) Joe is at the bar with his friends. Since he has some money that is burning a hole in his pocket he says to his friends, "This round is on me...drink up." Needless to say, that is exactly what his friends do. They order the best (most expensive) drinks in the bar. So much for Joe's extra money. As a matter of fact the tab is so large, Joe has to spend more than he originally planned.

2) Susie is at a bar with her friends. She also has some money burning a whole in her pocket. However, Susie only plans to spend half of her money. She's still focused on saving for her car. Susie tells her friends, "Hey guys I have an extra ____ dollars, anybody want anything from the bar?"

Who sounds more like you? You see it is not usually about the money itself. It is about your thoughts on how you should deal with the money that is contributing to your money issues. If we can recognize the flaws in our use of these common myths, notions, and sayings, then we can adjust our thinking (consciously and subconsciously) and consequently our behavior in dealing with money. We can then move forward in solving our financial issues.

What you just read was an example of how I processed a saying that I felt represented a negative "-" OUTLOOK about money. Consider this, neither that saying nor any of the sayings is either positive or negative. It is the fact that I classified the saying as a negative in my mind that made it an issue that needed to be addressed.

Peeling back that onion

The next step is for you to analyze the sayings you marked as negative. Yes, I want you to analyze each and every one. Focus on why you feel that way. Follow the worksheet below as an example and from your TOTALS line above include enough lines for each of the "-" NEGATIVE OUTLOOK towards money you marked.

Here is an example of how I analyzed a saying (fig 1.2):

SAYING # 11 "Money burning a whole in my pocket."

Worksheet 2 - Analysis

Saying #	Question: What is the money "doing"?	Reason you feel it is negative (analysis)	The positive rewrite
11	Is the money really burning me?	It makes me feel I must spend it quickly	Money burning a whole in my pocket means I have money!

Fig. 1.2

Wow, imagine that! Money burning a whole in my pocket means I have money. Well that is absolutely true, when you think about it. Now, what was your money issue you wanted to solve? You know, the reason you picked up this book in the first place. Guess what? You have just identified money to use towards solving that issue. Doesn't that make you feel good? It definitely makes me feel good sharing these concepts with you.

Time to grab your pencil again - I want you to answer these questions in your analysis:

Take that first saying you marked with a minus "-".

1. Why did you mark it with a minus "-"?
2. Did the money do anything or is it something you've heard or believed and just accepted?
3. What exactly did the money "do" in the saying you chose? Is the "money" actually doing something or forcing you to do something?

ANALYSIS: Why do you feel it represents a negative OUTLOOK towards money? (What is it that makes it negative?) How could you turn this negative into a positive?

POSITIVE "+" REWRITE: Rewrite the saying to make it positive.

By doing this exercise you begin to work on yourself at a subconscious level. Every time you hear the saying you will automatically recall the positive it offers because you made it that way. You will subconsciously begin change the way you approach solving money issues.

CHAPTER 1 SUMMARY

To wrap this chapter up and bring it home...

The purpose of this chapter is to teach you to "re-think" how you think about money by presenting you with a list of myths, notions, and sayings. Using those sayings you learned to:

a. Identify those, which you feel, are negative "-" and those that you feel are positive"+", enabling you to become more aware of the influence of the sayings.
b. Focus on those you identified as a "-" NEGATIVE ATITUDE, which helped you to begin to address the source of some of your OUTLOOKs and behaviors towards money.
c. Develop the following WORKSHEETS:
1. SAYINGS
2. ANALYSIS

This exercise forces you to change what you felt were negatives into something you created and made positive. That once negative notion is now, not only a positive in your mind but begins the process of training your mind to take any issue and focus on the positive and the possibilities that come with it.

With an open mind and a positive outlook, there is no money issue you cannot solve. As you move to the next chapter and the rest of the book remember the following:

By taking this: STEP ONE -YOU have set the stage for success!

CHAPTER 2 – IDENTIFYING YOUR PROBLEM

Not a day goes by where there isn't something tugging at our financial resources. You either want or need something or worse someone else wants or needs something and looks at you to provide it. Usually we casually dismiss these wants and needs and we categorically lump them all into the melting pot of "our" problems.

"Dude, what's your problem?" How many times have you ever heard that in your life? There is always somebody asking you about your business. Well, maybe you should answer the next person that asks you that question. That's right, just go ahead and give them a piece of your mind. Tell them what it is that is troubling you. Then see how fast they try to get away from you. The truth is no one wants to hear your problem. Yeah, they always ask, but they really don't want to know what your problems are. They have too many problems of their own. Who wants to add to their problems by listening to yours? That's not to say that there aren't caring people out there willing to help you solve your problems…but they usually come at a price.

Well, when it comes to getting organized to solve your financial issues the most important question really is…

Dude (or dudette), what's your problem?

However, no one is asking you this important question but I really care about your answer and that's why I wrote this book. The person who should be asking this question is you! This is absolutely the most important step you will take in reading this book. It is the reason why you are reading this book in the first place, whether you realize it or not. Until you can specifically articulate what it is you need or want to fix, when it comes to your finances, can you even begin to tackle the task of actually doing something about it.

Dude, What's Your Problem?

This chapter is about identifying issues, period! I will show you how to identify, categorize, and gain awareness about the personal problems that may be hindering your financial freedom. Let us get started shall we? I hope that you kept that pencil handy if not go grab it. Don't even sigh! You know how it goes…anything worth having or doing is work. The good news is that you only have to do this once. Once you know how; you know how forever! On a sheet of paper, I want you to write the words MY PROBLEMS. (fig 2.1)

Worksheet 3 - My Problems

Problem #	My Problems	What happpens when I solve my problem?
1	I need a new car	I can get to work on time
2	Pay off credit cards	I have one less bill
3	I'm overweight	I'll feel and look great!

Fig. 2.1

Next comes the fun part. Start writing down your problems. I mean all of them. If you have an issue write it down. From… "My car is a piece of junk." to "My credit card payment is over due." I want you to list all of your problems. Anything you can think of write it down. I don't care what the issue relates to just write it down. This is one of those incidents where the more the merrier really is true. Now you can cheat and only write down a few so you can get on to the next step but you'll only be limiting yourself in the long run. Come on just keep writing. I'm not going anywhere we can pick up right where you left off at anytime. Take a couple hours or days if that is what it takes but write down all the problems you have or think you have. Gotta nice list? Good, lets move on to the next step.

Life Would Be So Much Better If Only...

The next thing I want you to do is get another piece of paper. On that paper at the very top I want you to write the question, "WHAT HAPPENS WHEN I SOLVE THE PROBLEM?" Now go get your list of problems. I want you to place your list of problems right next to this new piece of paper. Take a deep breath and look at your first problem. On the new piece of paper with the question, "WHAT HAPPENS WHEN I SOLVE THE PROBLEM" I want you to start answering that question for each problem you listed. (fig. 2.1)

Here let me give you an example.

On my list, my very first problem was that my car doesn't run. So on my "WHAT HAPPENS WHEN I SOLVE THE PROBLEM " paper I wrote... I can get to work without walking or riding the bus. Wow, it is that easy. You don't need to write out a detailed explanation just a simple statement. Let's do another one. The second thing on my paper was that I needed to pay off my credit card. So on my WHAT HAPPENS paper, I wrote... I'll have one less bill to worry about. It's just that simple.

Now you go ahead and continue through your list. I'm going to go grab a soda and some chips... Be right back!

I'm sure, by now; you are wondering what is the purpose of this exercise? This exercise specifically allows you to see past your problems. It allows you to visualize what will be once you solve your issue. Now you have a subconscious path leading from what your problems are to how things will be after those problems are eliminated. So now what is left for us to do? That's right, actually solve the problem and that is what this book is all about. So have you gone through all of your problems? Well if you have...good for you. If you haven't keep working on it, however the show must go on.

A Place For Everything...

I now want you to go get a sheet of paper and place these headings on it (fig. 2.2). I would like you to place the heading "FINANCIAL", the heading "RELATIONSHIPS" and the heading "OCCUPATION". To make it easier, I will define the categories:

• FINANCIAL. List all of the problems you have that deal with money or a lack thereof. This is all the things that you feel can be solved on a purely financial basis.
• RELATIONSHIPS. List all of the problems you have that deal with relationships with others. This also includes any relationship problems you may also have with yourself. Example: "I think I'm overweight." Addictions also fall under this category.
• OCCUPATION. This is where you can list all of your problems that are associated with your job or profession.

Worksheet 4 - Categories

FINANCIAL	RELATIONSHIP	OCCUPATION
Problem #	Problem #	Problem #
2	3	1
4	8	6
7	9	5

Fig 2.2

What you are going to do now is go through your list of problems from WS 3 and place them under the category you feel is most appropriate. If you feel some of your problems could be placed in more than one category then feel free to place it under more than one category. An easier way may be to just list the problem # from WS # 3 under the appropriate category instead of rewriting the entire problem.

The purpose of this exercise is two-fold. First, it makes you aware of what you feel your problems are. It may prompt you to think of more problems but it can also make you aware that what you thought was a problem is in reality inconsequential. The second thing this does is allow you to get a sense of how big or small your problems really are. Up to now, if you are like most people, and me, many times we just lump everything together in that melting pot of problems. Well that pot, at times, can grow very large fairly fast and become very overwhelming and hence the major source of our concerns and well being. By placing your problems in categories, you allow yourself the ability to attack your problems in small manageable pieces. As the saying goes… "The best way to eat an elephant is one small bite at a time." This exercise allows you to do that.

Once you complete your categorization you have already made a significant achievement! You have listed all of your problems and placed them where they are most relevant to you. Most people can never solve any of their problems because they cannot articulate what they are. Go ahead, pat yourself on the back; this is a great SECOND STEP! Take a good look at your list. Read it up and down. Do you notice anything? Actually, you probably notice a whole bunch of things. What I want to bring your attention to is the importance of the problems in that list. Do you notice that although you have a random list, there are certainly some problems in that list that are significantly more important to you than some of the others?

At this point, we are going to focus your efforts. You are going to work on the problems under the category, "FINANCIAL". It is not that the other categories are not important, quite the contrary, however, I feel the majority of the other problems can usually be traced back to an issue which is rooted in not enough cash in the bank to pay all the bills. It is only appropriate to begin working on your cash flow problems first.

Who's on first, what's on second?

I guess you probably have an idea of the next exercise. The next exercise is for you to prioritize your "FINANCIAL" problems list (fig. 2.3). I want you to look at each of the problems and decide if the one below it is more important to you than the one you are currently looking at; if it is more important, than move it ahead of the current problem. I want you to continue in this manner until you have prioritized your entire list. In no time at all you will develop a nice and ordered list. Now things are beginning to come together. Now take a good hard look at your list. What you have before you is golden. Before you is a list of all of your financial problems, sorted in terms of importance to you. If you stopped reading this book right now and never read another word, you have one of the most important things you will ever need to help you solve your financial issues. No matter what approach you may take to solve your financial problems you now know what they are and have an idea of what order they need to be solved. That is a very important document to have in your possession. A document you created. As good as this list is, however, it is missing one important component, which will make it even more powerful!

Worksheet 5 - Financial Problems

FINANCIAL	PRIORITIZED FINANCIAL
Problem #	Problem #
2	7
7	13
13	30
18	2
23	24
24	18
30	23

Fig. 2.3

The "Pucker" Factor

One of the most elusive elements in this universe, which we will never be able to control, must be added to your list. That element is the "ELEMENT OF TIME". As powerful as your list is, it is still incomplete. The element of time makes all of the difference!

Let me take a moment to illustrate how important the "ELEMENT OF TIME" is to your list. On my list the first problem is the fact that I need a car. That is the most important financial problem I have---according to me. My second problem is I need money to pay my electricity bill. The way my list is organized, the problem I need to focus my attention on is doing whatever it takes to get a car, but lets add the element of time. Between my two problems, which do you feel is going to affect me quickest -- figuring out a way to acquire a vehicle or my lights being turned off because I failed to pay the bill? The addition of time to the equation really shakes things up. What may be important in one sense may be of lesser importance when you must factor in how fast you need that problem solved.

Once again it is time to do another exercise. I would like you to re-prioritize your FINANCIAL list based on the "ELEMENT OF TIME." (fig. 2.4) The problems you feel you need to solve sooner rather than later should be moved to the top of the list. Other problems, though important but can be pushed off until later, will be placed further down on the list. Remember, time is money and you need to make the most of the time you have available to solve your problems. Priority is the key. Once you have prioritized your list you are finished.

Worksheet 6 - Time based financial problems

PRIORITIZED FINANCIAL LIST BASED UPON THE ELEMENT OF TIME
Problem #
13
7
2
23
18
30
24

Fig. 2.4

"BREAK TIME"
Whew, you've earned it!

The Million-Dollar Question

Although you are essentially finished with this chapter I am curious to know what you are doing now to solve your problems and why it isn't working for you? I assume your methods aren't working simply by the fact that you have this book and are working through the exercises presented. Anyway, I am just being nosy but it would be interesting to know. If you just wrote down all of the things that seem to get in the way or keep you from "getting ahead", that too would be a start in the right direction. Like they say in the military…

> "It's hard to cross a minefield if you don't know where the mines are."

If you take the time to write down what is getting in your way, you will have an easier time getting around those obstacles. It also helps when you can see those obstacles. Sometimes you just won't be able to avoid them but at least you see them coming and can brace yourself for the impact.

CHAPTER 2 SUMMARY

We are about to get into the meat of this book in the next chapter, but first I want to take this time to sum up all of the things we discussed in this chapter. You should be wiped out. We covered a lot of ground. I promise you this is by far the hardest section in the entire book, at least mentally. The hard work is behind you. It is all down hill from here. So let's review what we accomplished in this chapter by creating all those lists.

a. We developed a list of problems. We wrote down every problem we felt we had.

b. We answered the question, "WHAT HAPPENS WHEN I SOLVE THIS PROBLEM?" for each problem we listed.

c. We created three categories: RELATIONSHIPS, OCCUPATION and FINANCIAL

d. We placed our problems under what we felt was the appropriate category for that problem. After that, we put aside the categories RELATIONSHIPS and OCCUPATION to focus on the FINANCIAL category.

e. We prioritized the problems listed under the FINANCIAL category, which created a potent list.

f. We added the element of time to the prioritized FINANCIAL list, which made it even more powerful.

g. We wrote down a list of things we felt were getting in the way of solving our problems right now. Basically, we marked our minefield so we now know where not to step if at all possible. That in a nutshell, is the path we have created so far.

h. Finally, we developed the following WORKSHEETS:

3. MY PROBLEMS
4. CATEGORIES
5. FINANCIAL PROBLEMS LIST
6. TIME BASED FINANCIAL PROBLEMS LIST

Congratulations you have just accomplished:

STEP TWO!

ARE YOU READY?

CHAPTER 3 - LEARNING HOW TO ORGANIZE

All right everybody hang on to your hats. We are now about to get into the heart and soul of this book. This is the reason why you picked this book up in the first place. This is where the rubber meets the road. This is where I tell you HOW!

Ladies and gentlemen, we are going into the construction business, not literally but figuratively speaking. I want you to get a mental picture. I want you to close your eyes and imagine driving up to an empty, abandoned lot. Your job is to build something. What are you going to do? What are the steps you are going to take? I'd reckon one of the first steps is to ask your boss, what the heck it is you are supposed to build. How can you even start if you don't know what to build? How do you order supplies? How do you know who to hire and when? Everything hinges on this, the most important issue. What are you building? Well guess what? We know what we are building. We are building a path to financial freedom. In the last chapter we took that all-important second step. We identified our problems---we know what we are building---a way to solve those problems. Now that we know what we are building, what's next?

In this chapter you will learn how to organize. I will identify the tools that are needed to begin organizing. I will also teach you how to use those tools. Finally we will wrap things up with a few exercises. Alright everyone, let's put on our hard hats and roll up our sleeves ---we've got work to do!

Tools of the Trade

There are two things that must be procured for our construction project. The first thing we need to get are supplies. In order to build we must have our bricks, our sand, our lumber, our nails and so on and so forth. The same holds true for building our path toward financial freedom. Here is a list of supplies you will need:

INCOME
Paycheck stubs – all of them
Other types of income stubs – all of them
Bank statements

EXPENSES
Account statements & cash receipts - all of them
Checkbooks - all of them
Monthly bills (utilities, credit cards) - all of them

Now as far as tools go here is what you need to procure:
Pencils
Pencil sharpener
Eraser
Notebook
Calculator
Optional but highly recommended: A Computer and Financial software
That's it! That is the list of things we will need to begin building.

For those of you who have computers and personal financial software – you will save yourselves time and writing cramps in creating the lists necessary in the upcoming exercises. For you, creating the lists will be a matter of keystrokes and I urge you to take full advantage of the technology available.

For those of you with a computer, but no software, if you have bank accounts that can be accessed on-line, contact your local branch office and find out what program(s) your account can be directly downloaded into. I recommend you purchase it, making sure to purchase the version required. This will be money well spent. If there is none, I suggest you take a quick look at the section about financial software packages. I recommend you choose a software package, install it and get familiar with it. It will save you time and writing cramps each month.

Taking Back Control

Now, take out the notebook. Before we begin I want you to write on the first page of your notebook, "TODAY IS THE DAY I START TAKING CONTROL OF MY FINANCES!" sign and date it. Starting today, this book and its exercises will show you how to take control of your expenses and how to make intelligent choices with your money. Wow, isn't this a great day to begin? Now take a deep breath...

INCOME

Now the first thing I want you to do is locate your INCOME:

- Paycheck stubs – all of them
- Any other types of income statements

These are very important. These indicate how much money you have coming to you that you can use to live your life. This is not an infinite number. You will learn how to live your life within that limited span of resources. If you have several jobs then you need to include all of your pay stubs. If you get paid in cash you still know how much you are getting paid.

DEFENSE FINANCE AND ACCOUNTING SERVICE MILITARY LEAVE AND EARNINGS STATEMENT

ID	NAME (Last, First, MI)	SOC. SEC. NO.	GRADE	PAY DATE	YRS SVC	ETS	BRANCH	ADSN/DSSN	PERIOD COVERED
	COMER DENNIS T		O4	870517	18	888888	ARMY	4809	1-31 MAY 05

	ENTITLEMENTS		DEDUCTIONS		ALLOTMENTS		SUMMARY	
	Type	Amount	Type	Amount	Type	Amount	+Amt Fwd	.00
A	BASE PAY	5900.90	FEDERAL TAXES	868.92	LONG TRM CARE	96.04	+Tot Ent	7942.89
B	BAS	183.99	FICA-SOC SECURITY	365.86			-Tot Ded	1926.68
C	BAH	1858.00	FICA-MEDICARE	85.56			-Tot Allt	96.04
D			SGLI FOR 250,000	16.25			=Net Amt	5920.17
E			TSP	590.09			-Cr Fwd	.00
F							=EOM Pay	5920.17
G								
H								
I								
J								
K								
L								
M							DIEMS	RETPLAN
N							830820	HIGH 3
O								
	TOTAL	7942.89		1926.68		96.04		

Pay Stub

On the next page of your notebook write, "WHERE IT COMES FROM MONTHLY". Under that heading, I want you to begin listing all of your sources of income, (fig. 3.1). Don't skip any sources. If you get some money from a job or for doing something list it. If you are married, cohabitating or share income/expeditures with someone then you must add the amount they are giving you or contributing to the income stream. In order to make this easier to work with – as you list each income, total what you earned for each month and write one line per month. Don't forget to include income that is only earned once a year. The last thing you should do to ensure you capture all of your income is to check your bank statements each month for any income deposits.

The first column on the worksheet is the "WHEN" column. We will use that column to track how often or when you had an income item. This will also help us later on, when we begin sorting the expenses. I want you to determine the "WHEN" using the following codes: [D – daily, W – weekly M – monthly, Q – quarterly, Y – yearly, X – extra]

Now I know there is no such thing as extra money, but we will use that for things like, winning a bet from a friend or the office football pool, or finding money in the washing machine...you know stuff like that. Oh yes, you need to be tracking all of your sources of income, until it becomes second nature.

****Oh, before I forget we must establish a time reference to track income and expenses. We will use monthly as the reference. Since most of us are paid monthly wages and receive our bills in monthly installments, it is the logical choice. All that means is that you must convert any daily, weekly, quarterly or yearly income or expenses into monthly ones. It's not rocket science just simple math. Worksheet 7 shows how you can convert the other time references into monthly ones****

Worksheet 7 - Where it comes from

WHEN	WHERE IT COMES FROM	D(aily) X 30	W(eekly) X 4	Q(uarterly) / 3	Y(early) / 12	M(onthly)
M	Paycheck (Job 1)					$1200.00
W	Child support		$250.00			$1000.00
X	Birthday					$50.00
W	Paycheck (Job 2)		$100.00			$400.00

Fig. 3.1

Have you written down all of your sources of income and their amounts? Good, now on to the expenses...

EXPENSES

Next, I want you to pull out, hunt up, and/or print off of your computer the following:

- Account statements & cash receipts - all of them
- Checkbook(s)/Register(s) - all of them
- Monthly bills (utilities, credit cards,.etc)

Transactions – (from computer based software, sorted by category, if available)

BOA-checking: Register

Date	Number	Payee/Category/Memo	Payment	Clr	Deposit	Balance
5/11/2005		State Farm	48.00	R		3,238.58
		Insurance:Life				
5/18/2005		Interest Earned		R	0.15	3,238.73
		Interest Earned				
5/18/2005		Balance Adjustment	1,970.00	R		1,268.73
		[BOA-checking]				
5/26/2005		HOUSTON'S 770.512.706 03/30	80.00			1,188.73
		Dining Out				
6/1/2005		DFAS-IN IND, IN ARMY ACT			5,900.00	7,088.73
		Salary				
6/1/2005		Bank of America	129.05			6,959.68
		split				
6/1/2005		USAA Federal Savings Bank	720.60			6,239.08
		split				
6/1/2005		Sprint PCS	122.00			6,117.08
		Utilities:Telephone				
6/1/2005		Verizon	34.00			6,083.08
		Utilities:Telephone				
6/1/2005		Comcast	64.00			6,019.08
		Utilities:Cable TV				
6/2/2005		Flagstar Bank	648.36			5,370.72
		split				
6/3/2005		Wells Fargo Home Mortgage	330.13			5,040.59
		split				
6/7/2005		STRANO & ASSOCIA CASH TRANS			645.00	5,685.59
		Rental Income:413 N. Virginia				
6/25/2005		DISCOVER SMART CHK	3,100.00			2,585.59
		Category	▶ Open Split			

Record Restore Balance Today: $2,585.59

Checkbook Register

On the next blank page in your notebook: I want you to write the words:

"WHERE IT GOES"

Pick up your checkbook and begin writing down a list of all the entries that you made in your checking account (see examples below). Of course I am making the assumption that you recorded all of your entries in your checkbook register. You need to do this for all the transactions made in your register for the past 12 months. From your receipts (I know you kept them) don't forget to include the items you paid with cash.

EXAMPLE # 1 If you purchase a specialty item on a regular basis (coffee, cigarettes) write the total.
Coffee – Feb. 1st $ 15.00
Coffee – Feb. 22 $ 10.00

EXAMPLE # 2 During the month of Feb. you went to various grocery stores for a total of 6 times ($20, $8, $80, $10, $22 and $100)
Grocery's - Feb. 1st $28.00
Grocery's - Feb. 5th $8.00
Grocery's – Feb. 12 $80.00

EXAMPLE # 3 Write each time you pay rent or a mortgage payment, even if the amount is the same. Rent $650.00

Your entries should look similar to fig. 3.2. Notice it has a "WHEN" column also? However, for our expenses/transactions we've modified the codes. For expenses, I want you to use these codes in the "WHEN" column:

[D – daily, W – weekly M – monthly, Q – quarterly, Y – yearly, SO– special occasion, and E -emergency]

Worksheet 8 is different from worksheet 7. We will still use the frequency column, however we will place the transaction cost in the column of the month it occurs. This allows you to see how you are spending your money each month throughout the year.

Worksheet 8 - Where it goes

When	Payee	Jan	Feb	Mar	Apr	May	Jun	Jul	Aug	Sep	Oct	Nov	Dec
M	Sprint	$25											
D	Starbucks	$3											
Q	ex wife (alimony)	$600											
W	Safeway	$50											
M	Wells Fargo Mtge		$1000										
Y	City of Burke		$500										
D	Quick Lube			$25									

Fig. 3.2

I understand that a year is a long time and your list will be very long but it is imperative that you stick with it and complete this exercise. The reason being is that there will be some expenses which will be seasonal. Christmas, for instance is a time when people spend a little more than they normally would. Birthdays and family traditions will also incur costs. The point is you want to write all of your transactions so that you can easily identify trends, reoccurring bills and other items. After you write down transactions for a few months it will be apparent which bills occur monthly, quarterly, etc.

On the next blank page in your notebook write:

"BILL ACCOUNT STATEMENTS"

I want you to do the same thing as you did on the previous worksheet (fig. 3.3). Write down the bill and the amount you spent for the past 12 months if you've managed to keep your statements. If you have been keeping accurate records in your checkbook register, many of these account statements will already be accounted for in your previous (expenses) list. This is a good way to establish a checks and balances system. You can check how well you've been recording your checkbook transactions by matching them up with the amounts on your bill statements. You may notice that you have bill/account statements that you can't find in your expense list. That usually happens when you forget to pay a bill. This exercise shows how easy it is to overlook a bill or two and the importance of getting organized to take back control!

Worksheet 9 - Bill account statements

When	Payee	Jan	Feb	Mar	Apr	May	Jun	Jul	Aug	Sep	Oct	Nov	Dec
M	Virginia Power	$25	$25	$25	$25	$80	$90	$90	$90	$45	$25	$25	$25
M	City Water	$15	$15	$15	$15	$45	$45	$45	$45	$15	$15	$15	$15
Q	ex wife (alimony)	$600			$600			$600			$600		

Fig 3.3

Now I know there are some of you who are just twiddling your thumbs because the last part didn't apply to you. I know, you guys didn't write down your transactions in your checkbook register nor did you keep any of your bill statements. You just paid them and threw the statements in the trash or just threw the bill statements in the trash and failed to pay them. If either of these situations applies to you, then shame on you.

However, good news, you now know what you need to do! The first two chapters can only take you so far. We are now in the building phase of our project and we must have the proper tools and supplies. Your checkbook transactions and bills are your tools. Until you have the tools to build you cannot go further into your project. If you have thrown your bill accounts or statements away, I suggest you find out if your accounts are available online. If yes, you can download past statements and transactions from the web site.

However, if not, this is a good time to start gathering and keeping your bill statements as well as a good time to start recording all of your transaction in your checkbook register. When you take cash out of the ATM keep track of these expenses also. Many times it is the little items that eat away at your income. In no time at all, you will have enough transactions to continue on with this exercise.

CHAPTER 3 SUMMARY

Let's review what we accomplished in this chapter:

a. We developed a list of supplies.
b. We developed a list of tools.
c. I taught you how to use those tools and supplies.

d. We developed a list of our INCOME and EXPENES. We wrote down all that we felt we had of each

e. We learned that we need to keep all cash receipts, account statements and bank statements.

f. We discovered why we need to record ALL transactions in our check register.

g. We created the WORKSHEETS:

7 WHERE IT COMES FROM
8 WHERE IT GOES
9 BILL ACCOUNT STATEMENTS

Congratulations you have just accomplished:

STEP THREE!

TAKE A BREAK!!!!!!

CHAPTER 4 -SORTING 101

Alright, let's get back to work. For those of you who have listed about a years worth of transactions we are about to take the next step. We are going to sort through your list

OK, in your notebook we need another sheet of paper (fig 4.1). On the top line write the headings:

DAILY; WEEKLY; MONTHLY; QUARTERLY; SPECIAL OCCASION; EMERGENCY

Begin now by listing each of the transactions where you spent money (EXPENSES), from the previous exercise (WS 8) under its appropriate heading. The purpose of this exercise is to once again give you an idea of what your biggest financial transactions are and at what times they occur. This is beneficial information and you will use this information a little bit later.

WS 10

Daily		Weekly		Monthly		Quarterly		Special		Emergency	
Exp	Amount	Exp	Amount	Exp	Amount	Exp	Amount	Exp	Amount	Exp	Amount
Star-bucks	$ 3	Safe-way	$ 50	Sprint PCS	$ 25	Ali-mony	$600	Vegas	$1000	engine	$600
Quick Lube	$ 25	.	.	Mtge	$1000	prop-erty tax	$259	B'day	$ 50	.	.
.	.	.	.	.	.	.	.	.	.	.	.
.	.	.	.	.	.	.	.	.	.	.	.
.	.		.	.	.	.	.	.	.	.	.

Fig 4.1

I'm going to go watch the news – be back soon, Take your time.

The purpose of this is to give you a "short" list of all of the transactions (bills) that occur MONTHLY. After you have done this for the transactions continue this process until you have gone through all of your headings (D, W, M, Q, SO, & E).

EXAMPLE: Over the course of 12 months, you have probably paid your rent (or mortgage) 12 times. Well, you only need to know that you have that transaction one time. If the rent has gone up list both amounts and if you have paid late fees (or NSF check fees) list them as a separate amount.

RENT JAN – MAR $ 500.00
RENT APR – DEC $ 550.00
RENT FEES MAY $ 25.00

Before we move on we have to get our hands around the "unaccounted" for transactions. Undoubtedly, in your first exercise going through your list of transactions and categorizing them under the headings D, M, Q, Y, SO and E; there were some transactions (things you spent money on) that just did not fall under any of those headings. These are things that may have happened only once. This would include things like going out and playing Bingo when a friend came to visit. It may be that occasional piece of furniture that you couldn't pass up. The fact of the matter is, there are times when you spend money because you need or want to. I want you to list all of the transactions that have not been listed under any of the other categories under special occasion (SO).

What came first the chicken or the egg?

You should now have six (6), "short" lists (columns) of all your transactions.

Four (4) of those lists contain transactions that occur during a specific time period:

DAILY, WEEKLY, MONTHLY, & QUARTERLY

Two (2) lists contain transactions that occur under special circumstances:

SPECIAL OCCASION & EMERGENCY,

The next step is a repeat of an exercise you have completed before. You are going to prioritize the 4 columns that are associated within a specific "TIME ELEMENT" – D, W, M, and Q. Go through each of these 4 columns and place a number "1" next to the most important "TIME ELEMENT" transaction in that column. Continue numbering the transactions until you have prioritized them all. Once you complete this exercise for these four categories we will move on to the next step.

EXAMPLE # 1: Your daily bus fare expense may be an important expense you have, but it may not be as important as the daily "childcare" expense.

EXAMPLE # 2 - An expense such as cable TV. It is important, but is it more important than paying the electricity bill due monthly? These are hard questions but they are not impossible to answer.

Basically, you are now getting down to the point where you will have to decide what is more important. You now have four (4) prioritized columns. However, you must now learn to work with them all together. Some of your daily transactions may be important as far as daily expenses are concerned but not as important as compared to a monthly expense.

At this point, you will take a different approach. You have before you four prioritized columns of your transactions. You are going to have to use those lists both independently and together. As we move into setting up a budget based on the information from all of the exercises, you will learn how to focus on the things (transactions) that are most important at a particular time and how to defer or delay those transactions that can hopefully be paid later.

Invasion of the money snatchers!

The next thing I want you to do with your four columns is to look through each of them very carefully. I want you to eliminate any transactions in those lists that are not absolutely necessary. For instance you may have lunch as a daily expense. Do you really need to eat out for lunch every day? Can you start bringing your lunch to work? That will eliminate that expense altogether and free up money to pay more important expenses.

Once you have eliminated all the transactions you feel you can, you have one last thing to do. We need to grab the calculator and total up the lists - all six of them. It is just as important to total up how much money you have spent on SO and E as well. You will see that these two categories of expense can be just as much as the first four categories combined. These two categories represent the majority of your discretionary expenses. With the exception of EMERGENCY transactions, which most of the time can't be helped, the other category of expenses are things you can do without or at least reduce your spending on. Do you have to send everybody presents on special occasions? Why? Are those presents more important than you gaining financial freedom? You must be able to help yourself before you can help others. Did you really need that new couch you listed under SO?

Have you totaled up all of your columns? Now it is time to do some of that same type math we did earlier. (Fig 4.2) How much money are you spending for SO,and E? Are you surprised? If you are not you're one of few. Most people are literally appalled when they realize how much money they are actually spending unnecessarily. No, I'm not talking about those transactions that must be paid daily, monthly, weekly, or what have you. I'm talking about the five bucks here for that double foam latte and twenty five bucks there spent going out drinking with the boys. Over time those small expenses add up. You now see how much those small things have cost you of your precious dollars "MONEY SNATCHERS"!

WS 11

Daily		Weekly x 4		Monthly		Quarterly / 4		Special /12		Emergency / 12	
Exp	Amnt	Exp	Amnt	Exp	Amnt	Exp	Amnt	Exp	Amnt	Exp	Amnt
coffee	$ 3	grocery	$ 125	Sprint PCS	$ 25	child support	$900	Vegas	$1000	car issues	$600
Quick Lube	$ 25	hair styling	$ 100	Mtge	$1000	vehicle tax	$259	B'day	$ 50	.	.
drinks	$ 50	.	.	car note	$ 500	land tax	$300	.	.	.	.
.	.	.	.	.	.	.	.	.	.	.	.
totals	**$78**		**$225**		**$1525**		**$859**		**$1050**		**$600**
month equiv	**$78**		**$900**		**$1525**		**$364.75**		**$87.50**		**$50**

FIG. 4.2

As I said earlier, this chapter is the meat of the entire book. These exercises represent the hard work that must be done in order to put you on a path towards financial freedom. Remember, you know where you came from...those are the problems we listed in earlier chapters. You also know where you want to go...that was the list of how things will be different when you solve those problems.

Well this is the "How to" part...the steps you must take to get started towards the destination (FINANCIAL FREEDOM). The best part about all of this is once you have completed the exercises you are well on your way. The hard work is behind you. As you keep track of your transactions over time you will begin to make smarter decisions with your money. You will begin to reduce or eliminate unnecessary expenses. Why, because you know what they are? You will begin to allocate money to the things that are most important. You will soon discover that you have money you can use to start or build up a savings. All of these things will become available for you as we go into our last exercise.

The sky is NOT the limit

Our last exercise will be to develop a budget. You have already started to do this by completing the earlier exercises. This is where you will bring everything together. The first thing I want you to locate is the sheet, "WHERE IT COMES FROM" (Fig 7). That sheet represents all of the money you make. Now take out your calculator and total up how much money you make if you have not done so already. Be careful to ensure you total your dollars in the appropriate time sequence (monthly). The point is you need to determine what time period works for you and convert all of your expense transactions in terms of that time period. I recommend using the monthly time period because most expenses occur monthly, however, use what works best for you.

Now you know how much money you have to work with (your limit)! The next step is to go back to your list of transactions labeled under D, W, M, Q, SO and E. (Fig 11). You need to total up these transactions if you have not done so already. I'm sure you are wondering what to do with the totals under the categories SO and E. I suggest the first thing you should do is add up costs of each column if you have not done so already. Once you get a grand total divide that by 12. That will give you a figure that represents how much money you spend monthly on Special Occaision "stuff". Though you probably can't do much about the transactions under E you do have a good idea on how much you can and need to reduce your SO spending habits. If you followed the exercises you should have monthly equivalents for all of the columns expenses. Hopefully the totals of your columns do not exceed your income. If they do don't worry. It just means you need to eliminate or reduce some additional expenses. However, because you have prioritized you now know what you can eliminate or reduce. The final step in this process is for you to compare WS 7 with WS 11.

Worksheet 7 - Where it comes from

WHEN	WHERE IT COMES FROM	D(aily) X 30	W(eekly) X 4	Q(uarterly) / 3	Y(early) / 12	M(onthly)
M	Paycheck (Job 1)					$1200.00
W	Child support		$250.00			$1000.00
X	Birthday					$50.00
W	Paycheck (Job 2)		$100.00			$400.00
total						**$2650.00**

Worksheet 11

Daily		Weekly x 4		Monthly		Quarterly / 4		Special /12		Emergency / 12	
Exp	Amnt	Exp	Amnt	Exp	Amnt	Exp	Amnt	Exp	Amnt	Exp	Amnt
coffee	$ 3	grocery	$ 125	Sprint PCS	$ 25	child support	$900	Vegas	$1000	car issues	$600
Quick Lube	$ 25	hair styling	$ 100	Mtge	$1000	vehicle tax	$259	B'day	$ 50	.	.
drinks	$ 50	.	.	car note	$ 500	land tax	$300	.	.	.	.
.	.	.	.	.	.	.	.	.	.	.	.
totals	**$78**		**$225**		**$1525**		**$859**		**$1050**		**$600**
month equiv	**$78**		**$900**		**$1525**		**$364.75**		**$87.50**		**$50**

WS 7 represents all the money you make in a specific time period - namely monthly ($2650.00). WS 11 represents all the money you spend converted to a monthly basis ($3004.50).

If you subtract your monthly expenses from your income you will get a number. If that number is negative, I want you to multiply that number by 12. The result represents how much you are digging yourself in a hole every year!

($2650.00 - $3004.50) = - 354.50 x 12 = **(-$4254.00)**

That number represents your high credit card bills and other debts. That number is the very reason why you never seem to get ahead or caught up on your bills. However, you can fix this situation right now! You have all the information you need right in front of you. If you are spending more than you make, then you need to scratch out some more unnecessary transactions from WS 11. It is called belt-tightening, doing without...living beneath your means! Until you make a committment to spend less than you make you will never achieve financial independence. You've come this far and did all of these hard exercises, you may as well put this information to good use. So on to setting up a budget.

Your objective in creating a budget is to keep your spending (expenses) less than the amount of money you make. Not only do you want to spend less but you also want to be able to put money aside for those emergencies that crop up from time to time. Since you already have a list of your expenses under the categories D, W, M, Q, SO, and E all you need to really do now is determine how much money you can afford to spend for each expense.

EXAMPLE # 1: Under your M category you probably have a rent or mortgage expense. Well that expense is fixed. You cannot eliminate it nor can you reduce it (unless you move). You know you must pay that expense from the money you make (your income).

EXAMPLE # 2: How about your electricity expense? That is a monthly expense. You may not be able to eliminate it but can't you reduce it? Can you turn off lights or not run the air conditioner as much, like during the day when no one is home? What about installing a thermostat and programming the hours it can run? Sure you can, you just have to decide to do it.

All you need to do is limit how much money you are going to spend in each expense and do everything you can to not spend more than that. This is all you have to do!

Now I know it is easier said than done but that's the whole point. Obviously, what you have been doing, if anything, is not working. It is time for a change and that change will begin now! All it involves is a little discipline and organization. I am providing the organization but the discipline is going to have to come from you.

As the old saying goes, Rome was not built in a day…you too will steadily progress over time. You may not be able to stick to your budget in all of the categories at all times but you must at least try. As time passes you will become accustomed to "living with less" or within/beneath your means. That is when true financial freedom will begin.

Neo, welcome to the Matrix

Now, are you getting tired of doing all of these things manually? I mean getting out the notebook, writing down list after list of transactions, expenses or what have you? If you are like most people this gets old rather quickly. Remember in the beginning of this project when we were listing our tools, there were two tools that I highly recommended. One of the tools was a computer and the other tool was some financial software. The reason I put you through this whole set of exercises was to get you used to what it takes to make a change and the level of pain associated with getting organized. However, the other reason we have been doing these exercises manually is that many of you reading this book will not have access to these advanced tools and I wanted to let everyone know that this can be accomplished with simple tools. You don't have to have any technology to start down the path of financial freedom. I will be perfectly honest, technology does help this process, just like it helps us in other areas of our lives but it is not a necessity.

COMPUTER PROGRAMS

For those of you that do have access to a computer we will continue. The first thing you must do is choose what type of financial software package you wish to use. There are many software packages available such as Microsoft Money®, Quicken®, and others. I have not found one program to be any better than any other. They all essentially offer the same functions. The biggest differences in software packages are the "bells and whistles" each provides. Regardless of which software package you choose there are some functions I think necessary for your package to have, these include:

• Import/export functions – the ability to bring in data from other sources into the software and the ability to take the information the software creates and use that in other applications. Of specific importance is the ability to import data from online accounts. Nowadays, almost every bank, credit union, credit card, and merchant has the ability to place your account information on the Internet. A user id and password is all you need to connect to your accounts online and see where you stand. Most of these online accounts allow you the opportunity to "download" those transactions from the website to your computer. Imagine if you will, if you downloaded your check account information directly into your computer. You will no longer be relegated to typing every transaction in manually. Another added bonus is that you will not have to worry about forgetting to record transactions in your check register. Believe me, your bank will record every transaction you conduct, whether you remember to record it in your own register or not. It is a simple way to do checks and balances.

• Check register functions –the ability to create a checking account where you can track all of your expenses. The program should allow you to fill out amount, payee, check number, etc as if you were filling out a paper check.

•Loan functions – the ability to create and set up loans for your purchases (home, vehicle, school, etc).

• Budget functions – the ability to create and manipulate a budget. A good feature in a software package is the ability to automatically create a budget based on the "checks" you write using the check register functions.

• Calculators – your software should not only have a basic calculator built in but the ability to compute loan amortization, yields for securities, home affordability and insurance costs just to name a few. You may not use all of these immediately but eventually you will learn the use of all of them.

• Tax planning functions – The ability to take your transactions both income and expense and project future taxes. Most of these features allow the user to change his/her status and see how different scenarios provide results.

• Report generation – The ability of your software package to present the information in a variety of ways is key. Suppose you want to know how many checks you wrote in a specific month. Most packages have a method to sort data by dates, times, payee's, cleared checks, categories, etc. Most of these packages also present data graphically, so you can get a visual picture of your spending habits.

• Tax return due April 15 – The above features will cut the amount of time (and possibly the expense if you use a tax service) in creating your 1040 tax return.

These are but a few of the many features these financial software packages provide but are the ones I feel are most important. The greatest function these financial software packages provide is the ability to integrate all of the information in all the separate functions into one highly manageable tool.

All you need to do now is to complete the Worksheets! The exercises are just the beginning. You must refine a process that makes it easy for you to stay on the path. In no time, you will see your financial issues slowly disappearing and as those financial issues disappear so will some of the issues in those other categories such as "RELATIONSHIPS" and "JOB/OCCUPATION". Amazing isn't it? As you develop your system of organizing and managing based on the information you've created in the exercises, you will begin to live within your means, because you know what those means are; you will be able to avoid financial pitfalls because you know how to identify what is coming next; you will know what transactions must be paid and when and which ones can be deferred.

"BREAK TIME"

CHAPTER 4 SUMMARY

Let's review what we accomplished in this chapter:

a. We took our transactions (expense) and we placed them in categories

b. We prioritized our categories based on time

c. We learned about the "money snatchers" and how to elimintate them

d. Created these WORKSHEETS:
10 SORTED EXPENSES
11 SORTED EXPENSES (MONTHLY EQUIVALENT)

Congratulations you have just accomplished:

STEP FOUR!

CHAPTER – 5 THE LANGUAGE OF MONEY

You know what, we're going take a break building and I'm going to introduce you to one more concept. That concept is what I call the LANGUAGE OF MONEY (LOM). The LOM is nothing more than your financial vocabulary. By learning new words and learning the meaning of those words, you will increase your vocabulary. Think about different jobs and professions. Doesn't each profession have a language unique unto itself? I mean doctors and lawyers don't speak in the same everyday language as electricians in doing their jobs. The point is, every profession has a language of its own and money is no different. There are terms and concepts that are used with money that will allow you to understand and manage it better. How can you communicate if you can't speak the language?

Homework???

Well, this chapter is dedicated to some exercises that will allow you to increase your financial vocabulary and the concepts associated with money. So how do I want you to start? Well, I want you to grab the remote control and turn on the television. Go ahead and grab a cold one if that suits your fancy. Now tune into one of those financial news networks. You know, CNBC, McNeil-Lehrer Business report, MSNBC or some other financial news station. So what are you hearing financially? What are the correspondents and reporters reporting? Are you hearing the words Dow Jones, earnings, unemployment, consumer price sentiment, interest rates, mortgage refinancing, building permits, housing starts and the list goes on and on?

This, my friend is the the **language of money!** Just like you learn the English language so you can read and communicate, these words must become a part of your daily vocabulary. No, I don't want you going up to your friends saying, ".... did you know the average retail sales for Home Depot this quarter....", but I do want you to know what it means and think of how you could use that information. That is the **first exercise**...watching television, easy huh?

The **second exercise** is for you to read. What do you read? The answer to that is anything and everything that is associated with the markets and the financial/economic industry. Read magazines, journals, books and everything else you can get your hands on. I recommend you start by just reading the business section of your local newspaper. I would also suggest you pick up Kiplinger's Personal Finance Magazine, Fortune Magazine and Money Magazine. There are plenty of others but those are some good ones to begin with. I suggest another step in getting started would be to write down a list of the terms and phrases you hear on the television finance and news channels. Take that list and using the greatest marvel of technology, the Internet, do a Google or Yahoo search on the terms. You will get more "hits" than you will know what to do with. Reading will make you aware of things as they happen around you. I'm about to get a little hokey on you but please bear with me. Just as we started this whole entire process by opening your mind to the possibility of change, the exercises of watching the financial news channels and reading financial stuff helps accomplish the same thing. You are going to be amazed at how quickly things that you didn't even notice before, you are now aware of. However, in the case of money and finances you are going to become aware of strategies and tidbits of information that will help you along in your journey to financial freedom. Who knows you may be going through the real estate section of your local newspaper and come across an awesome article on purchasing a house. Normally, you'd just skip over it thinking to yourself one day I will own a house. However, now, you are actually going to cut out that article because you may not be ready right now, but you know that is one of your goals and you now have a path to get there. Call me crazy but that is exactly how the mind works once it has been exposed to new things and new possibilities. Don't worry, you'll be thanking me later and with that I bring a close to this very short but necessary chapter.

CHAPTER 5 SUMMARY

Let's review what we accomplished in this chapter:

a. We talked about the Language of Money and how it can help us on our road to "FINANCIAL FREEDOM"
b. Homework – watch the financial channels.
c. Homework – read anything and everything that is associated with the markets and the financial/economic industry.
d. We wrote down terms and phrases

Congratulations you have just accomplished:

STEP FIVE!

INTERMISSION – CAN I TALK?

It is once again time to take another break. This time I want you to head to the fridge, grab something cold to drink and lay back in the recliner. I'm just going to talk for a moment, or rather you are just going to read. No pressure, this is strictly for the heck of it. My feelings won't be hurt if you just skip this section and go to the next chapter, however, since you have some free time....

Did you know the average consumer credit card debt is now hovering near $10,000 and that is up from $8,500 just a few years ago? Did you know that America is facing record property foreclosures? Did you know personal bankruptcy filing is no longer considered something shameful, but has become something "necessary" to keep our economy afloat? Do you know that ***we are all paying*** for this each and every day?

When someone goes out and ruins their finances to the point that they must file bankruptcy, we all get to share in bailing that person out. Yes, you and I both pay our hard earned wages to let that person start all over. Think about this. You go out and over extend yourself on credit card debt. You buy TV's, vacations, clothes, vehicles...you name it you buy it. When you buy these items, you help the company that made the product make money (a profit). The company uses some of that money to pay bills and to pay employees. Those employees turn around and spend their money just like you do on the things they wish to buy, thus the cycle continues and our "economy" keeps going.

When Joe Knucklehead gets in over his head, he quits paying. Well the company still has to pay those salaries to the folks who work to make the products Joe bought, however the company didn't get all its money because Joe Knucklehead didn't finish paying. So guess what? Some employees may get laid off! The company has put people out of work because they can't afford to pay employees if others won't pay them. Now those folks, who just got laid off can't afford to pay their bills, the cycle continues and bankruptcies rise... everybody loses! What happens with the bankruptcies? Well those people get to start all over again, with zero debt. They usually don't owe anybody anything, nor can anybody go after them to make them pay once the court has made a judgment.

Now, the penalty for filing bankruptcy and getting yourself in trouble is to put a black mark on your credit report (black mark = bad credit or credit risk). That mark tells everyone that you are not trustworthy to pay your debts on time and it is risky to lend you money on credit---you deadbeat! So what, who cares? Companies are in the business of making money, they don't care about your riskiness, they want to get some of your money any way they can and they have many ways to do it.

First of all, companies and businesses will just charge you more for the product you wish to buy if you have bad credit. Where one person with no black marks pays $45 for a chair on credit, you are going to pay $90 for that same chair on credit. Why, because the companies and businesses are betting that by the time you "quit" paying your payments on the chair, you will have already paid at least $45, which is what the chair is worth in the first place. If you pay all your payments then the extra money is theirs to keep because they took a risk that you would not pay in the first place. Remember, your bad credit is an indication you are not trustworthy to pay. So how does everybody pay for Joe Knucklehead? In higher prices! Stores, companies, manufacturers, everybody who has something to sell just charges more for their products and services. They want to make sure they charge enough money to compensate for all of the Joe Knuckleheads and they know there will be plenty of Joe Knuckleheads (those who do not and will not pay their bills on time)!

So there you have it. Now you can understand why a book like this is so important. To prevent you from becoming a knucklehead or becoming a knucklehead again! You see one of the main problems with the economic system, as a whole is there is no mechanism to teach people how to manage money in the first place so we don't get into certain financial situations.

The second part of that is once people do get in trouble and we bail them out through bankruptcy is that they still don't get any help/counseling and people go out and do the same thing again. It is a vicious cycle. Now some would argue the system is set up that way to keep business going, so business can keep producing jobs, thus stimulating the economy. That's what they say, I'll let you be the judge. Just ask yourself how many jobs could be saved if the CEO wasn't being paid millions of dollars or stealing millions of dollars? This is something you need to think about. As costs for everything rise, because they hardly ever go down, how are you going to manage the limited money you make to accomplish your goals? That is the question we will tackle in next chapter…Goals!

CHAPTER 6 – GOALS

As always, we must start with a summary of what we have accomplished:

- We identified a list of common sayings and notions toward money.
- We learned how to identify our negative feelings towards money and change those feelings into positive feelings we can use.
- We identified our problems with life in general and specifically our problems with money.
- We learned what tools and supplies are needed to organize and manage money and we learned how to use those tools.
- Finally, we organized our finances in such a way as to quickly identify our shortfalls and how to manage them.

My question to you is this: Even if you successfully did everything I have instructed so far, would you be happy?

- Yes, it is the start of a program that you can follow for a lifetime.
- Yes, you would be living beneath your means.
- Yes, you would be solving your financial problems and you would have more freedom than you have now.

But again I ask, would you be happy? What would it accomplish? My point is it is all well and good that you have now developed a plan, a path so to speak towards that island of financial paradise but how do you know when you have arrived? Well earlier we did describe how life would be once our problems were solved and I guess that is close enough. Well, then I guess a more important question is how do you measure how far down the path you've gone? The only way, my friend, to measure your success is to develop goals that help you get to your ultimate destination.

EXAMPLE: How would you plan a road trip for a family vacation?

First, you would get a map to determine a path. You would need to know where you are starting from and where you are going. Secondly, you would set goals. You would determine how many miles you wanted or needed to drive each day to reach your destination. You would create a flexible plan. If you need to get to your destination quicker, you adjust your goals accordingly. You keep achieving those goals until finally you look up and you have reached your destination.

Surely you have experienced being lost...where you thought you knew where you were going. You took a wrong turn somewhere, drove around for a while and suddenly realized, you no longer knew where you were, nor how you got there. Some of us are able to figure it out after a period of time; others have to go ask for directions.

Goals are like life's mile markers. They let you know how far you've traveled and let you know how far you have to go. Without these goals, you would have no direction; you would have no purpose. Taking a journey down the path to financial paradise is just like driving. You must have goals (mile markers) set out in advance or you will find yourself lost on the path, knowing where it is you want to go but not having any way of measuring where you are and how far you have to go. I used to ask my friends why they went to work. The most common answer was...to pay bills! I would follow up with a so what? We all have bills to pay. I would ask, "what does going to work everyday accomplish?" More often than not, my friends would pause and then give me specifics like...pay a mortgage, daycare expenses, my car payment and cell phone bill must be paid...you know, the usual stuff. I would listen to their answers and nod my head in agreement. Then I hit them with the whammy! I would ask, "so at what point do you know you have enough money where those bills are not a concern?" I would pause for a moment and then I'd hit them with the second punch. I would follow the first question up with, "How much money do you need and for what"? I usually got nothing but blank stares and irritated facial expressions. I quit asking my friends these questions because quite frankly they were embarrassing and put people on the spot. I have come to the conclusion that most folks can't answer the questions because they just do not know the answer! People go to work everyday, earn money and subsequently spend it without much thought. It is what we do. We go to work to pay bills, day after day, month after month and year after year....all for what? That leads me to believe the old saying, "People don't plan to fail...they fail to plan" is as valid today as it has ever been. The first step in developing a plan is to have some goals, remember, 'life's mile markers'? So without further ado, it is time to get out your notebook one last time to complete our final exercises. (fig. 6.1). I want you to begin writing down the things you want to accomplish in your lifetime. I want you to write down things like purchase your own home, send your children to college, learn how to water ski, climb Mt Everest! List whatever it is you think will make you happy in the future.

Worksheet 12 - Goals

Goal #	My Goals
1	Purchase a home
2	Climb Mt Everest
3	learn to water ski
4	send my kids to college
.	.

Fig 6.1

Next, I want you to pick out just one of your goals. It doesn't matter which. As my goal I'll choose, 'Purchasing my own home'. Now under your goal, I want you to list all the things that you need to accomplish that goal. (fig 6.2) For my goal, I would list things like saving money for a down payment, figuring out what type of home I want (ranch style, two story, condo, townhouse), how many bedrooms and bathrooms. Those things I just listed become my mile markers. As I work towards figuring some of those things out, I know I am that much closer to achieving my overall goal of purchasing my own home. The biggest factor I see in my goal is saving money for the down payment. Remember, we developed a way of managing money earlier. You already prioritized your expenditures and you know where you can cut corners. My question to you is: How important is this goal? Can you make the hard choices to get you there? As you progress and begin to live beneath your means, you too, can begin allocating money specifically for your "down payment" goal. You may set a sub-goal to contribute $150 a month towards your down payment. In no time at all, as you stick with your plan you will soon have enough money to make the down payment.

Worksheet 13 - Steps towards my goal

Goal #	Things I must do to accomplish my goal
1	Save money for a downpayment
	Pick out a type of house
	Decide where I want to live
2	Get in shape
	Learn to Hike

Fig 6.2

A Soldiers Story

Let me tell you one of my personal stories. A job transfer moved me from the Midwest to the east coast, Belleville, IL to Alexandria, VA to be exact. I drove my cool F250 4x4 pickup towing a hot corvette. While I in Belleville, I had purchased a modest 3-bedroom home with a two-car garage; my mortgage was about $700.00 a month. Boy was I in for a rude awakening! My apartment rent, oh yes, I said apartment, not house, in Alexandria was $1600 a month! That was for a 1,250 sq ft, 2 bedrooms, 2 bathrooms, and living space…no garage; underground parking was $75 per vehicle, so add another $150 to the rent. Why was I in that apartment in the first place you ask? Well, because the average price for a "shack" in Alexandria at that time was well over $375,000! My house in Belleville cost me $80,000! I could not afford to buy an 'out-house' in the northern Virginia or D.C. metro region. That is two states and one district that I could not afford a house in which to live. Well, I take that back. I could afford a house if and only if I wanted to spend 1 – 3 hours on the road commuting each way, depending on traffic congestion. Have you seen the traffic congestion in D.C. and northern Virginia? I made the trade off for time and convenience but paid for it in the cost of rent. Anyway back to the story. I also had a rental property, which happened to go south! I had to evict some tenants for consistently being late with their rental payments.

I was stuck with two vehicle payments (cool truck and hot corvette) a mortgage payment and rent! Well, I needed a vehicle so one car payment was justified. It was the additional $500 truck note and the $1,100 "empty" house mortgage payment that were the issues. Now don't get me wrong, my income was enought to afford making all those payments (I was living beneath my means). I was not in a bind but living was very tight. I didn't have any money left over to do anything else, least of all afford a down payment for a new home. So I had to make a decision. Did I really need the truck? I never drove it except on the occasion to buy some furniture from IKEA or to help someone move. I was spending $500 a month in truck payments, not to mention the associated costs of insurance, registration, and gas.

Why did I really need it...so that I could help somebody move? I had the same issue with my empty rental house (utility bills, insurance, property taxes). So guess what, I bit the bullet and sold them! The next month after selling the house and truck, I paid my bills as usual but this time I had a lot more money left in my checking account than I was used to. I had an extra $1,600 a month! I was used to not having that money, so I made the decision to save $1,200 a month towards a down payment for a home. The other $400 I just added to my partying fund. An extra $400 buys a lot of brew and munchies, not to mention a trip or two to Baltimore's Inner Harbor or Atlantic City. It did not take long at all to save up enough money to make a nice down payment.

...and the point is...

My point is, my goals drove my actions and life drove my goals. I did not plan to move to Alexandria, the Army transferred me there for my next assignment. I didn't plan to sell my truck and house, but my goal of home ownership drove my actions to do so. Uh, oh, I'm about to get philosophical here but life is nothing but manageable, organized chaos. You never know what life is going to throw at you next. As such you have to be prepared to adjust at any given moment. In terms of finances, once you get a plan like the one you are developing using this guide, you have the ability to adjust to any situation life presents. By having goals established early you know that if you get bumped off your path to financial paradise, you know where you are and that you may have to go around an obstacle or two but that you will be able to get right back on your path. Remember your goals will change over time, as they should because life changes and because you are accomplishing those goals, one by one...checking them off. As you accomplish a goal or it no longer a priority you just move on to the next one, plain and simple. So my friends, you know what you need to do. I believe I have given you all that I have to offer on this particular subject. Go out and achieve all that you desire out of life, with the comfort of knowing you have developed a **personal** system of organizing and managing finances. Good luck, Godspeed and God Bless you for doing all you can to not be a knucklehead!

SO WHAT?

CONCLUSION - So what does it all mean?

Absolutely nothing if you don't take this information and use it! Sorry folks, from here on out you are on your own. Here is something to consider though. How about looking at this from a sports perspective. I can think of no greater exhibition of amateur sports than the Olympic Games. During the Olympics, all we can talk about is how many gold medals the United States athletes won in respect to the other nations. There we are all cheering on Marion Jones, Mike Phelps, the US basketball team and all the other teams and individuals. Yes, victory is sweet but what is even sweeter is having the ability to compete. Just making it to the Olympic games is no small feat by any means. However, what you don't see at the games is the countless hours of practice and training these athletes dedicate in preparation for competition. All we see is the product of that training, focus and dedication. All we really see are the results! You too are an amateur. You are an amateur at the game of personal finance!

Money Myths and Money Mistakes is your training manual and the beginning of your journey to financial freedom. This journey is going to be long and hard in the beginning. It is going to be time consuming and you will not want to do it. This is no different than anything else you want to accomplish in life…lose weight, become a doctor, help disadvantage children, become a foster parent. There will need to be changes made in your regimen and that will require a period of adjustment. You will either remain vigilant or you will quit! The choice is yours and yours alone to make a difference in your life.

There isn't an athlete in the Olympic games that does not have a "coach" pushing them to work harder. Giving them the guidance and skills to become even better than they ever thought they were capable. However, there is not one coach, who is willing to "spend" their personal time training an athlete, who has not exhibited neither the talent nor dedication to want better for himself or herself. It just does not happen.

So the same is true of your personal financial situation. If you do not exhibit the willingness to change your way of life and do the things necessary to take control no one is going to want to "coach" you. Yes, there are professionals, who get paid, to help others get back on the right financial path and if you are so inclined, you should seek one of those professionals. However, they can only give you information on the things you need to do. Success is up to you. So the all-important question is how motivated are you? Do you really want to win a gold medal in the game of life or do you really believe someone will just hand you a medal? Even if someone handed you a gold medal it would not mean a thing because you did not earn it. If someone asked you how you got the medal all you could say was that you asked for it and someone gave the medal to you, I believe that would be the end of that conversation. What else would there be to talk about? Conversely, if you worked hard to win that medal, you will wear that medal proudly because it will mean something to you. As you work to get your financial house in order, it will be an accomplishment you will be proud of. You can tell folks what it took to achieve it and you can teach others to do the same. You can show them the worksheets and explain to them how they helped you gain financial freedom. So why not be an inspiration to those that mean the most to you...your family, friends, co-workers, and church affiliates?

That, my friend, is what it all means…being in a position financially to help yourself and/or the people that mean the most to you, whenever you choose to do so. Can you now imagine what your life would be like once you have learned, practiced and adopted the ideas presented in ***Money Myths and Money Mistakes***?

• Can you imagine, never worrying about having enough money to pay bills?
• Can you imagine not having to worry about how you are going to send your children to college?
• Can you imagine not having to worry about where you will find money to save for a down payment on a new home?

I guarantee that if you apply the strategies of this book and stick to it, you won't be imagining any of this stuff. You will be living it! You have the book, you have the tools and you now have the knowledge, the rest is up to you. Do not spend your money on this book in vain. If you won't shatter the myths and take financial control for yourself, do it for those you care about and for those who care about you.

Once again, I bid you...Good luck, blessings and perseverance on your path to financial freedom.

WORKSHEETS

Worksheet 1 - Sayings

#	SAYING	+	-
1	A bird in the hand is worth two in the bush		
2	Money makes the world go 'round		
3	A fool and his money are soon parted		
4	Money is the root of all evil		
5	It's only money		
6	Money doesn't grow on trees		
7	Money doesn't bring happiness…		
8	Money can't buy love		
9	Money talks and BS walks		
10	Don't put all of your eggs in one basket		
11	Show me the money		
12	The buck stops here		
13	Don't throw a good quarter after a bad nickel		
14	A bad penny always returns		
15	Money burns a hole in your pocket		
16	Put your money where your mouth is		
17	Knowledge is power but money pays the bills		
18	Don't be penny wise and pound foolish		
19	Don't nickel and dime me		
20	Cash is king		
21	Another day, another dollar		
22	Money follows money		
23	Neither a lender nor a borrower be		
24	I got my mind on my money and my money on my mind		
25	Watch the pennies and the dollars will take care of themselves		

Worksheet 2 - Analysis

Saying #	Question: What is the money "doing"?	Reason you feel it is negative (analysis)	The positive rewrite

Worksheet 3 - My Problems

Problem #	My Problems	What happpens when I solve my problem?

Worksheet 4 - Categories

FINANCIAL	RELATIONSHIP	OCCUPATION
Problem #	Problem #	Problem #

Worksheet 5 - Financial Problems

FINANCIAL	PRIORITIZED FINANCIAL
Problem #	Problem #

Worksheet 6 - Time based financial problems

PRIORITIZED FINANCIAL LIST BASED UPON THE ELEMENT OF TIME
Problem #

Worksheet 7 - Where it comes from

WHEN	WHERE IT COMES FROM	D(aily) X 30	W(eekly) X 4	Q(uarterly) / 3	Y(early) / 12	M(onthly)

Worksheet 8 - Where it goes

When	Payee	Jan	Feb	Mar	Apr	May	Jun	Jul	Aug	Sep	Oct	Nov	Dec

Worksheet 9 - Bill account statements

Daily		Weekly		Monthly		Quarterly		Special		Emergency	
Expense	Amount	Expense	Amount	Expense	Amount	Expense	Amount	Expense	Amount	Expense	Amount

Worksheet 10 - Sorted Expenses

Daily		Weekly		Monthly		Quarterly		Special		Emergency	
Exp	Amount	Exp	Amount	Exp	Amount	Exp	Amount	Exp	Amount	Exp	Amount

Worksheet 11 - Sorted Expenses (Monthly Equivalent)

Daily		Weekly x 4		Monthly		Quarterly / 4		Special /12		Emergency / 12	
Expense	Amount	Expense	Amount	Expense	Amount	Expense	Amount	Expense	Amount	Expense	Amount
totals											
monthly equiv											

Worksheet 12 - Goals

Goal #	My Goals

Worksheet 13 - Things I must do to accomplish my goal

Goal #	**Things I must do to accomplish my goal**

ABOUT THE AUTHOR

When his father deployed, sometimes for several years at a time, Dennis Comer became the man of the house. A self-proclaimed military brat, he learned to organize and manage the household financial matters as early as age twelve. He utilized the discipline and organization of the military life to take advantage of the concepts of systemic investing and learned to recognize opportunity when it presented itself.

Dennis carried on his family military tradition by joining ROTC in college and subsequently going on to become a career military officer. Never one to overlook an opportunity he began investing in real estate all over the country taking advantage of the unique situations his various duty stations presented.

Dennis holds a B.S. in Computer Science from Prairie View A&M University and an M.S in Operations Research from the Florida Institute of Technology. He is currently serving on active duty as a military evaluator for the Army Test and Evaluation Command.

Dennis is currently pursuing a graduate degree in Publishing from George Washington University. His goal after retirement is to help others publish their dreams.

QUICK ORDER FORM

Email orders: piraas@mac.com

Fax: 703.717.0808

Postal orders: To order copies of Money Myths and Money Mistakes mail check or money order for $14.99* per copy to:

PIRAAS®
PO Box 3093
Alexandria, VA 22302

To make a **tax deductible charitable donation** and help financial literacy programs receive ***free*** copies of Money Myths and Money Mistakes, mail check or money order payable to

THREE TAYLOR'S VENTURES
c/o PIRAAS
PO Box 3093
Alexandria, VA 22302

For an electronic version of Money Myths and Money Mistakes in PDF format please visit our website at: www.moneymythsandmoneymistakes.com

Please send the following number of Books:

________ qty

Sales tax: please add 5.0% for products shipped to Virginia addresses

***Shipping by air**:
US: $4 for the first book and $3 for each additional product.

International: $9 for the first book and $5 for each additional product (estimate only).

Name:______________________________________

Address:____________________________________

City__________________ State________ Zip________

Phone____________________

Email Address:________________________________

Credit Card orders only available through PayPal
paypal email: piraas@mac.com

NOTES

www.ingramcontent.com/pod-product-compliance
Lightning Source LLC
Chambersburg PA
CBHW020210200326
41521CB00005BA/330

9780976740827